Sleepover Secrets

Wardrobe Makeovers

Stephanie Turnbull

A+

Smart Apple Media

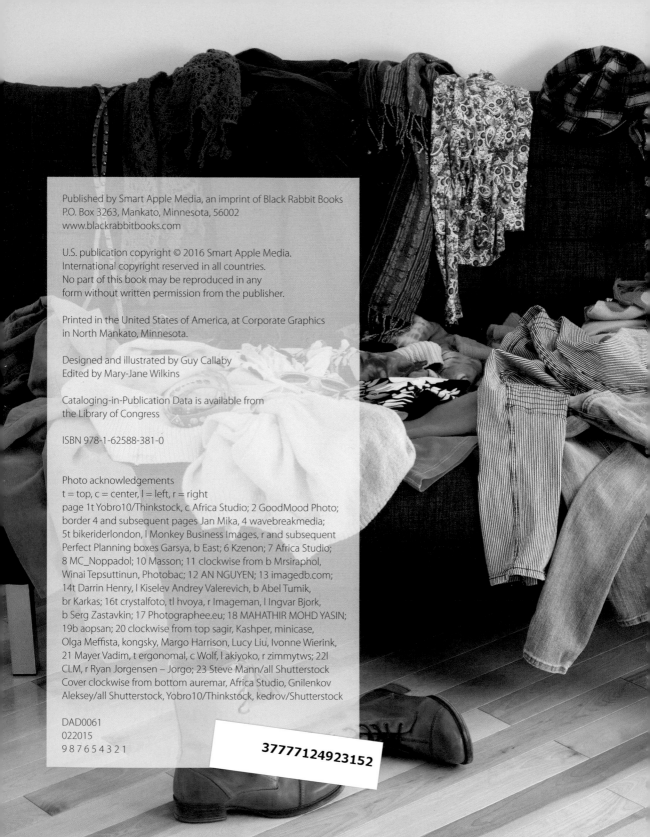

Published by Smart Apple Media, an imprint of Black Rabbit Books
P.O. Box 3263, Mankato, Minnesota, 56002
www.blackrabbitbooks.com

Printed in the United States of America, at Corporate Graphics
in North Mankato, Minnesota.

Designed and illustrated by Guy Callaby
Edited by Mary-Jane Wilkins

Cataloging-in-Publication Data is available from
the Library of Congress

ISBN 978-1-62588-381-0

Photo acknowledgements
t = top, c = center, l = left, r = right
page 1t Yobro10/Thinkstock, c Africa Studio; 2 GoodMood Photo;
border 4 and subsequent pages Jan Mika, 4 wavebreakmedia;
5t bikeriderlondon, l Monkey Business Images, r and subsequent
Perfect Planning boxes Garsya, b East; 6 Kzenon; 7 Africa Studio;
8 MC_Noppadol; 10 Masson; 11 clockwise from b Mrsiraphol,
Winai Tepsuttinun, Photobac; 12 AN NGUYEN; 13 imagedb.com;
14t Darrin Henry, l Kiselev Andrey Valerevich, b Abel Tumik,
br Karkas; 16t crystalfoto, tl hvoya, r Imageman, l Ingvar Bjork,
b Serg Zastavkin; 17 Photographee.eu; 18 MAHATHIR MOHD YASIN;
19b aopsan; 20 clockwise from top sagir, Kashper, minicase,
Olga Meffista, kongsky, Margo Harrison, Lucy Liu, Ivonne Wierink,
21 Mayer Vadim, t ergonomal, c Wolf, l akiyoko, r zimmytws; 22l
CLM, r Ryan Jorgensen – Jorgo; 23 Steve Mann/all Shutterstock
Cover clockwise from bottom auremar, Africa Studio, Gnilenkov
Aleksey/all Shutterstock, Yobro10/Thinkstock, kedrov/Shutterstock

DAD0061
022015
9 8 7 6 5 4 3 2 1

Contents

Time for fun!

Sleepovers are great fun, whether there are just two of you or a whole gang. If you all love clothes, a fashion evening will keep you so busy you won't want to go to sleep.

What to do

Hunt for old clothes and scarves to **customize**, or ask friends to bring **accessories** to swap. Or raid your dress-up box and wear the craziest things you can find!

Chill out!

Enjoy experimenting with style ideas but don't take it too seriously—it's not about who has designer labels or expensive jewelry. Don't worry about trying to look like movie stars or models in magazines—just relax and be yourself.

Glam up your evening with beads, sparkly hairbands, and feather boas.

Don't leave anyone out —make sure you're all having fun.

Perfect Planning

Find comfy cushions and provide snacks to keep everyone happy. Don't forget a camera for funny photos!

Mix and match

Ask everyone to bring a suitcase of clothes, then experiment with mixing and matching to create stylish combinations and cool new looks.

Raid your wardrobe for stuff to try on.

Get sorted

Sort everything into tops, pants, skirts, and dresses, then put different items together to see what works. Here are a few tips to help you.

1. Don't wear too many colors or patterns.

*Stick with similar shades, then add a **contrasting** T-shirt underneath for a splash of bright color.*

2. Mix your seasons.

Try wearing light, thin summer dresses with leggings or tights and a cardigan or sweater on top.

3. Go easy on the sparkle.

Team one eye-catching piece with plain items so it stands out (and you don't look like a Christmas decoration).

4. Create a balance.

Very tight or baggy outfits don't look great, so pair loose tops with skinny jeans, or clingy tops with wider skirts or trousers.

Perfect Planning

Provide coat hangers so clothes don't end up in a crumpled heap on the floor.

Designer tops

Be brave and use a pair of scissors to customize old, boring tops! You might create some daring new fashions.

1. Lay a plain, stretchy top on a flat surface. Draw a line with chalk about 2 inches (5 cm) from the side, then make small cuts in from the side, up to the line.

Make the snips about ½ inch (2 cm) apart.

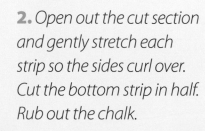

2. Open out the cut section and gently stretch each strip so the sides curl over. Cut the bottom strip in half. Rub out the chalk.

3. Now take the top strip and pull it over the second one…

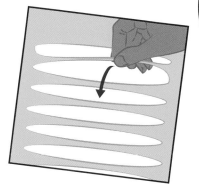

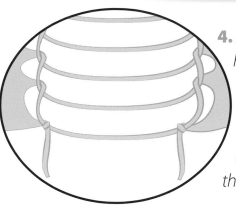

4. Pull the two halves of the cut strip through the last loop and knot in the corners.

… then take the second strip and pull it over the third. Pull the third strip over the fourth, and so on until you reach the end.

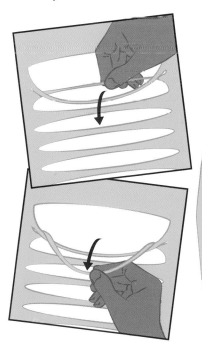

5. Repeat steps 1-4 on the other side, then wear it over a contrasting T-shirt to highlight your stylish slashes.

Perfect Planning

Look for cheap tops in thrift stores so everyone has something to cut up.

Scarf style

Scarves can make great fashion statements—around your neck, on hats, as belts, or knotted to a bag... there are so many things to try!

Colorful scarves go well with plain, simple tops.

Hair scarves

Long, thin scarves look great tied in hair. Grab one each and try these chic styles.

1. Smooth the scarf and tie it tightly at the side of your neck, keeping it wide and flat on your forehead.

2. Wrap the scarf up and over your hair, then cross the ends and twist them once, like this…

… then tie them at the back of your neck.

This creates a twisted band.

This neat look helps keep hair out of your eyes.

3. *Tie the scarf at the side of your head and twist the ends tightly.*

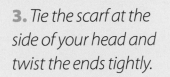

Hold the end of the twist and coil it around.

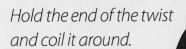

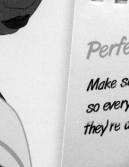

Tuck the end inside to make a funky flower shape.

Perfect Planning

Make sure you have mirrors so everyone can see what they're doing.

Scarf crafts

Liven up plain scarves with brooches, badges, or sewn-on buttons and **sequins**. Try threading shiny beads on to fringed scarves, or plaiting the strands.

Ribbon weaving

1. *Cut a piece of thin ribbon about the length of your scarf and thread it on to a **darning needle**. **Weave** it in and out along one edge of the scarf.*

2. *At the end, remove the needle and leave a length of ribbon dangling. Add more ribbon strips.*

Scrunchy scarves

Use the same weaving method to create a ruffled effect.

1. Thread a needle with thin elastic cord and tie a bead on the end.

2. Thread the elastic along one edge of the scarf, pulling so the scarf scrunches up.

Perfect Planning

Keep needles in a safe place so you don't step on them later!

3. Tie the elastic around another bead at the end and cut off any extra. Thread more cord up the middle and along the other edge.

Hair flair

Making hair accessories out of old jewelry, ribbon, or fabric is great fun. Use your imagination to design something stylish.

Clips and bands

Try attaching feathers, brooches, or fabric flowers to hair clips or grips to make eye-catching **fascinators**. Or how about sewing buttons or beads onto a thick, stretchy hairband?

Perfect Planning

Ask everyone to bring a hairband so you all end up with a clever hair creation!

No-sew bow

Find a thick ribbon or silky **sash** from a dress to make this neat hair bow. You don't need to cut it, so you can unravel it later.

1. *Fold the material over and over to make a fat roll about 4 inches (10 cm) long. Leave the last bit hanging.*

2. *Wrap an elastic hair tie around the middle to form a bow.*

3. *Wrap the loose end of the material once or twice around the hair tie, then tuck it under the tie at the back.*

4. *Pull out layers at each side to widen the bow. Poke a plastic hairband through the wrapped end at the back.*

Try fixing a sparkly brooch or earring stud to the middle of the bow.

Cool jewelry

Do you have boxes crammed with jewelry you never wear? Now's the time to lay it all out and have a look—and get your friends to do the same.

Mix and match

The key to wearing jewelry is not to pile on too much! Team one big, striking piece with several smaller ones—for example, a wide, chunky bracelet with dainty earrings. Mix and match jewelry with your friends to see what looks best.

You can always break the rules and wear everything at once!

Be inventive

Turn old accessories into new ones: a long necklace could be twined and knotted with another to create a great mix of colors…

… or it could be wound around your wrist as a bracelet…

… or even worn as a belt.

Perfect Planning

Buy thin, stretchy cord so you can take apart old necklaces or bracelets and thread the beads in exciting new combinations.

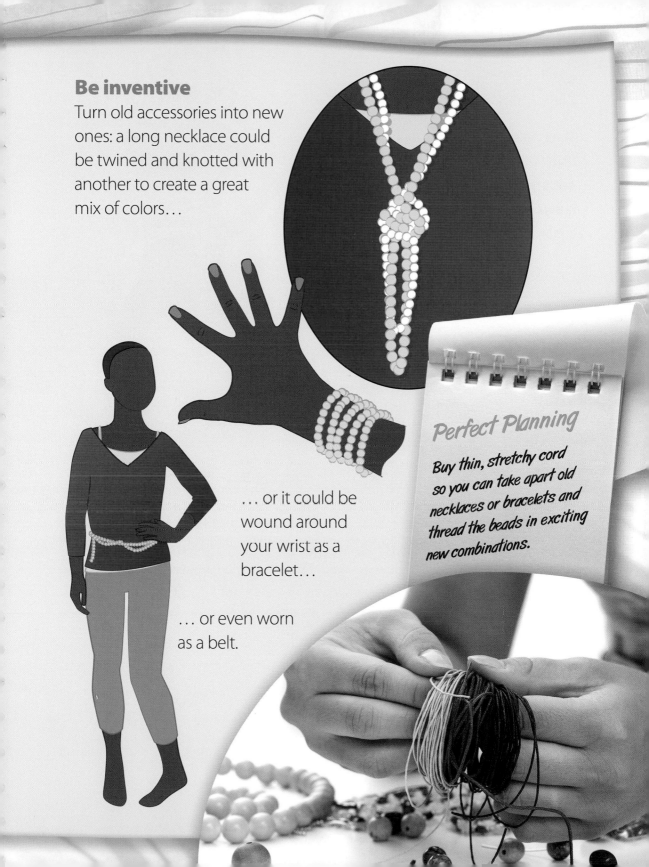

Brilliant bags

You're sure to have bags in your wardrobe, so try a bag-swapping session! You could also customize bags with badges, key rings, ribbons, or patches.

Denim pocket bag

Try this neat way of recycling pockets from old pairs of jeans into handbags.

1. *Cut out a back pocket with sharp scissors. Go up to the* **seam** *above the pocket to make a flap at the top.*

Don't snip any stitching around the pocket!

2. *Plait colorful cord or ribbon to make a long strap, then tie it in a loop.*

3. Lay the pocket face down. Fold back the flap and trap the strap underneath. Sew a few stitches down one side of the flap.

4. Carry on sewing across the bag to attach the flap to the back of the pocket. Don't go through to the front of the bag or you'll seal it! Finish with a few stitches up the other side as in step 3.

5. Decorate your bag with sewn or stuck-on buttons, **felt** shapes, plastic jewels, or sequins.

Perfect Planning

Find some plain cotton shopping bags and decorate them with **fabric pens**.

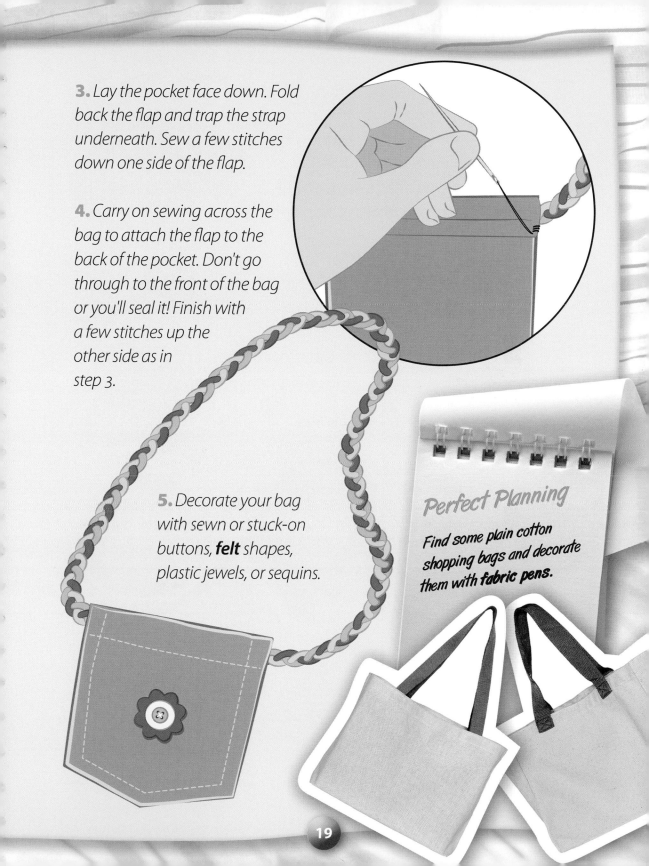

Love that hat

Hats are fun to try on, swap, and decorate. Help each other give old hats new life with a few carefully chosen accessories.

Summer chic

Sun hats are great for protecting your head on hot summer days. Personalize yours by clipping on small fabric flowers or brooches…

…or tying on a stylish scarf…

…or threading shells or beads on ribbon or cord.

Winter wool

Liven up a plain yarn hat by weaving ribbon in and out of the fabric, clipping on big, bold hair accessories, or gluing on sparkly gems.

Try making shapes from felt, fixing them together by sewing a button in the middle, then attaching a safety pin to clip it to your hat.

Perfect Planning

Clear a space in your bedroom for a catwalk to model all your stylish stuff!

Glossary

accessories
All the extras, such as jewelry, scarves, bags, hats, and belts, that you add to clothes to create stylish outfits.

contrasting
Looking strikingly different. Contrasting colors are ones that stand out well against each other, such as yellow and blue.

customize
To change something to suit you. Clothes and accessories can be customized to fit better, look more stylish, or create something new and exciting.

fabric pens
Pens specially designed to be used on fabric and not wash off. Be careful not to get the ink on your clothes by mistake!

fascinator
A fancy hair accessory attached to a comb or clip. Fascinators are usually made up of decorations such as beads, feathers, and flowers.

fascinator

darning needle

darning needle
A long, very thick needle with an extra-large eye (hole).

felt

Soft, thick fabric made out of matted, pressed wool. Felt is cheap to buy, easy to cut and comes in lots of great colors.

sash

A long strip of material, tied around the waist of a dress.

seam

The join where two pieces of fabric have been sewn together.

sequins

sequins

Small, shiny circles of plastic or metal with a hole in the middle for sewing on to clothes as decoration.

weave

To lace long threads together, going in and out.

Web sites

www.scarves.net/how-to-tie-a-scarf
Learn all kinds of different ways of tying scarves around your head or neck.

www.firstpalette.com/Craft_themes/Wearables/Wearables.html
Find fun ideas for making hats, bracelets, necklaces, and much more.

www.fashion-era.com
Read fascinating facts about fashion through history, from ancient underwear to modern trends.

Index